What's That Got To Do With Me?

War and Conflict

Antony Lishak

W

FRANKLIN WATTS
LONDON•SYDNEY

First published in 2005 by
Franklin Watts
96 Leonard Street
London
EC2A 4XD

Franklin Watts Australia
Level 17/207 Kent Street
Sydney NSW 2000

© Franklin Watts 2005

Series editor: Adrian Cole
Design: Thomas Keenes
Art director: Jonathan Hair
Picture researcher: Diana Morris

A CIP catalogue record for this book is
available from the British Library.

ISBN: 0 7496 6399 5

Dewey Classification: 327.1'6

Printed in China

Acknowledgements:
Lynsey Addario/Corbis: 8, 28cl, 32. Martin
Adler/Panos: 6cl, 18. Sally & Richard
Greenhill/Alamy: 26. David Grossman/Image
Works/Topham: 6c, 11. Atef
Hassan/Reuters/Corbis: 2, 7, 31. Manchester
Evening News: 14. Jeff Paterson: 10.
Photofusion/Alamy: front cover t, back cover t, 27
(posed by models). Jason Reed/Reuters/Corbis:
front cover b, back cover b, 2-3, 19, 29. Rex
Features: 9, 24. Alex Segre/Rex Features: 6cr, 13.
Courtesy of Sakue Shimohira and Nagasaki
Foundation for the Promotion of Peace: 20, 28c.
Sipa Press/Rex Features: 21, 23, 25, 30. Topham:
15, 17. US Pacifist Party: 22.

Contents

So what?

Imagine a world in which war and conflict do not exist. You can't, can you? The sad fact is that ever since stone-age men clashed over who should have the biggest cave, disagreement has been part of our lives. Today, there is little sign that things are going to change.

What's it all about?

The closest most of us get to armed conflict is when we watch a film. But in the larger world, disputes between governments frequently result in them sending their soldiers into battle. In this book you will meet a selection of people whose lives have been touched by war – a serving US Marine, the survivor of an atomic bomb and a child soldier. You will also hear about conflict on a more day-to-day level; from a victim of bullying and a computer war games fan.

Personal accounts

All of the testimonies are true. Some are first-hand accounts, while others are the result of bringing similar experiences together to create a single "voice". Every effort has been made to ensure they are authentic. To protect identities, a few names have been changed and models have posed for some of the pictures. Wherever possible, permission to use the information has been obtained.

Ask yourself

The testimonies won't tell you all there is to know about war and conflict, that wouldn't be possible. Instead, as you encounter the different views think about your own opinions and experiences. This will help you begin to address the question: "War and conflict – what's that got to do with me?"

For many people, like the Iraqis, armed conflict is part of their everyday lives.

A soldier

Thousands of soldiers choose to put their lives on the line in wars. Here, Major Tom Fisher explains why he is one of them.

I joined the US Army 14 years ago to help others. That's why I'm here in Iraq – so that these people can be free. And it's not all fighting. Success here is measured by things, such as the millions of people who have clean drinking water and how many schools are constructed. War is not just one big shoot-'em-up computer game. It's all about back-up and support; what the military calls "logistics". There's a whole network of people working as one big

Soldiers are professional; they are specially trained for battle.

Fact bank

■ During the last 3,400 years only 268 have been completely warless.

■ Over 108 million soldiers were killed in war and conflict during the 20th century.

■ In the 1990s alone, wars were responsible for the deaths of about 6.3 million civilians.

team – supporting each other. You know, over 5 million meals are served to the troops here in a single week!

But I don't want you to think it's a holiday camp out here. People die in war – there's no getting away from it. I've seen things that keep me awake at night, but my training helps me cope.

Flag-covered coffins of dead US soldiers.

If someone wants to shoot me he's got to expect me to stop him.

And it's true, sometimes the wrong people get killed; war has always been messy. However, in today's world, war is necessary. Sad but true. To me it's about good and bad, right and wrong. I believe I am on the right side.

Ask yourself this...

■ Do you agree with Major Fisher? Can war be right? Is there a right side and wrong side in a conflict?

■ What causes, or people, would you be prepared to fight for?

A conscientious objector

Conscientious objectors are people who feel it is wrong to fight. Sometimes soldiers, when confronted with the reality of war, realise that they just could not kill. This is one such soldier.

My name is Stephen Funk. I signed up as a US Marine Corps reservist, to serve in Iraq, when I was 19. I wasn't planning to join the military, but an army recruiter convinced me that basic training would give me a sense of direction in my life.

Stephen Funk spoke out against war, even though he had enlisted.

I soon discovered that the purpose of military training is to churn out non-thinking machines. I believe all humans have a natural aversion to killing, and being forced to shout out "Kill! Kill! Kill!" every day damaged my mind, body and soul. My revulsion towards violence grew stronger, but I was afraid to speak out. Then an instructor yelled at me that in a war situation I would be too weak to kill. His aim was to toughen me up, but without thinking I replied that he was right. It was like breathing out after holding it in for two months.

From then on I could not remain silent. I wanted others who may be thinking about enlisting to learn from my experiences. So I spoke out in public against the war. At first, some people told me I was a traitor and a coward – I even had a few death threats. However, I also received tremendous support, even from other enlisted men and women.

Anti-war protesters in the USA. Some people felt troops should not be sent to Iraq.

Fact bank

■ In March 2003, a US-led force of around 170,000 troops invaded Iraq. Following a long dispute they believed that the Iraqi president, Saddam Hussein, was developing weapons of mass destruction. Around 50 US reservists, like Stephen Funk, objected to the invasion. Stephen Funk was found guilty of desertion and spent five months in a military prison.

Ask yourself this...

■ What could the Marine Corps do to prevent people like Stephen Funk joining up in the first place?

■ When have you ever refused to do something because you felt it was wrong?

■ Who do you think deserves to be called a hero – Major Tom Fisher or Stephen Funk?

A computer games fan

Sam spends a lot of his life in war zones – on his games console. Scientists disagree on how much people are affected by what they play, or if they are affected at all.

I'm fourteen and I love computer games. And let me tell you, there's more chance of a duck-billed platypus becoming prime minister than there is of me becoming a crazed killer. It's just a game! If someone can't tell the difference between real life and fantasy, the problem's in their head, not on the screen.

Sam sees a clear difference between real life and fantasy.

In one game I collect points for not killing people, but helping them.

Fact bank

■ Some researchers believe war games that involve co-operation and teamwork between players could develop personal skills. Other studies have shown that violent computer games help children to channel their aggression in a safe way. However, biological research has found that playing a computer game for a long time causes similar chemical changes in the human brain as those associated with taking illegal drugs.

The same sense of what's right and wrong, that stops me from being violent in the real world, affects the way I play computer games.

Anyway, all these games come with safety guidelines and are rated so parents can see if they are suitable for their children. If a four-year-old has nightmares because he has seen someone's brains blown out in an 18-rated game, then it's the parents' fault!

Violent computer games, such as the one being played here, are often blamed for an increase in violent child behaviour.

Ask yourself this...

■ To what extent do you think that the games Sam plays on his computer are likely to make him a more violent person?

■ Why aren't young children allowed to play whatever they want on a computer, for as long as they want?

■ When have you been stopped from buying or playing a computer game, because someone thought it wasn't "suitable"?

A war veteran

What happens to soldiers when the fighting stops? Here is the story of an Argentine war veteran who served during the Falklands War in 1982. It seems that once war is over, enemies can become friends.

My name is Alejandro Videla – I was 19 years old when I was sent to fight against the British in the Malvinas (the Falkland Islands). We were badly equipped and didn't really stand a chance, and eventually surrendered to the British troops. As prisoners of war we were given hot food and clean clothes. We were just glad to be alive and desperate to go home.

After the cease fire, one of my comrades accidentally set off a bomb and was injured. Immediately, some

Alejandro Videla (left) with a British Falklands veteran on his visit to England.

Fact bank

■ In 1982 Argentine armed forces invaded the Falklands (a small group of British-governed islands). Britain sent their armed forces in response, resulting in a conflict that lasted 72 days and claimed about 1,000 lives. Argentina still lays claim to the islands they call the Malvinas, although the two nations are now at peace.

Discarded Argentine equipment after the war.

British soldiers came and took him to the field hospital. His life was saved by the same men who, earlier, were trying to kill him.

But life back in Argentina was hard. I had to stop watching football because the giant fireworks set off by the crowd reminded me of the explosives. Many of my friends felt the same, but we were not allowed to ask for help. The government prevented us from talking in public about the war.

Then I found a website for British war veterans and posted a question on the message board. I was contacted by one of the soldiers who helped my friend. He was finding life after the war difficult, too – at last we had someone to talk to who understood what we were both going through. When I came to visit him and his family in England, it was like finding a long-lost brother.

Ask yourself this...

■ Why do you think it helped Alejandro to contact a British war veteran?

■ How do you "make up" and trust someone again after you've had an argument?

■ Why do people forgive and forget?

Wartime technology

Some everyday things that we take for granted owe their existence, in part, to developments made during wartime. You just have to know what to look for, as this doctor has discovered.

My name is Dr Adrian Richardson and I have to admit, although I don't like it, that many aspects of my work and life have directly benefited from war. Penicillin, the medicine that attacks dangerous bacteria in our bodies, was successfully developed only during the Second World War (1939–1945). I'm certain that the way road accident victims are treated nowadays is down to the experiences of countless battlefield surgeons. That goes for the treatment of burns and the use of plastic surgery.

Dr Richardson believes there are some benefits to war.

All around my house are inventions that partly owe their existence to war. There's the microwave oven in the kitchen, the computer in my office and the smoke detectors in the hall. Then there are the satellites that tell us the weather, and form the network connections for the Internet and my mobile phone. And my trip to Japan last year would never have been possible without wartime [jet] research. Yes, like it or not, without war the world would certainly be a different place.

Ask yourself this...

■ Which of the items that Dr Richardson mentions would you find it most hard to live without?

■ How much do agree that, on balance, because of all the wartime medical advances outlined by the doctor, war is a good thing?

Sir Frank Whittle and his jet engine.

Fact bank

■ The medicine penicillin was first discovered by Alexander Fleming in the early 1920s. Howard Florey and Ernst Chain adapted his work almost 20 years later during the Second World War. Since then it has saved millions of lives.

■ Dr Hans von Ohain (for Germany) and Sir Frank Whittle (for Britain) are both considered the inventors of the jet engine. Dr von Ohain's engine powered a jet that first flew in 1939, followed by Sir Whittle's in 1941.

A child soldier

**Sometimes children are forced to fight.
Here is the disturbing story of one such child.
He is 12 years old and comes from Liberia.**

They came and took us at night – all the children in our village. One boy tried to escape, but he was caught. His hands were tied, and then they made the rest of us kill him with a stick. I felt sick. I knew this boy from before. At first I refused to kill him, and then they told me they would shoot me.

They pointed a gun at me, so I had to do it. The boy was asking me, "Why are you doing this?" I said I had no choice. I still dream about the boy from my village who I killed. I see him in my dreams, and he is talking to me and saying I killed him for nothing, and I am crying.

Child soldiers in Liberia. In some conflicts children are forced to bear arms.

Fact bank

■ The United Nations defines a child soldier as being under 18. There are some fighters in war-torn regions of the world who are as young as 8 years old.

■ There were about 100,000 child soldiers in Africa in 2004.

■ Most child soldiers are recruited by armed groups and not by regular government supported forces.

Child soldiers in Myanmar (Burma).

My job was to run out into the battleground and grab weapons, watches, wallets and any ammunition from the dead soldiers, and bring it all back. This was difficult. The enemy could see you and pick you off as you ran out and back again. I was given this job because I was the smallest. Sometimes when I fell asleep on sentry duty, I was beaten by my corporal. He beat me like a dog, like I was an animal, not a human being.

I could not run away. If they caught me they would kill me. And where would I go? At least if I stayed with my commander he would feed me and I would have somewhere to sleep.

Ask yourself this...

■ Why do you think children in some parts of the world are recruited to fight at such a young age?

■ How old are you? If you were forced to kill your neighbour, how do you think you might be affected?

■ Being part of an armed group gave this child access to food and shelter that he may not otherwise have had. Do you think it's worth the risks he took? What else could he have done?

An atomic bomb survivor

The atomic bomb is the most devastating of all weapons. There are enough bombs in existence to destroy Earth many times over. The only two that have ever been used during a war were dropped by the USA on Japan in August 1945. Sakue Shimohira witnessed the horrific effects.

My name is Sakue Shimohira. I was 10 when the atomic bomb fell on my town, Nagasaki. When the air-raid siren sounded I fled with my sister to the nearby shelter. My mum stayed behind to draw some water from the well. After a while the alarm was lifted and everyone got ready to leave. Then there was a sudden brilliant flash of light and I passed out. When I opened my eyes I couldn't believe what I saw. Some people were so horribly burnt that it was impossible to tell if they were men or women.

We began to cry hysterically; luckily my father found us and led us out of the shelter. The ground was littered with the dead and dying, and the air was thick with the stench of burning. When we got home we found my mum's body. The whole thing fills me with enormous rage and sorrow.

Atomic bombs keep killing long after they have exploded. Thousands of people who survived the blast died through radiation sickness, and for years many more suffered from illnesses caused by that terrible weapon. Even today, 60 years later, people suffer.

Sakue Shimohira survived the bombing.

Fact bank

■ Many people believe that after the Second World War, a nuclear conflict between the USA and the Soviet Union was prevented because there was a "balance of power" of weapons on both sides. Today, there are still over 20,000 nuclear warheads worldwide. Each of them is up to 10 times more powerful than the bomb that fell on Nagasaki.

■ Since 1947, the Doomsday Clock has been a symbol of how close the world is to nuclear disaster. It currently stands at 7 minutes to midnight (midnight is nuclear war). In 1953, it stood at 2 minutes to midnight.

A military parade in North Korea. North Korea is one of several countries thought to be developing nuclear weapons.

Ask yourself this...

■ Do you think nuclear weapons act as a deterrent? What would happen if every country had them?

■ Is it right to wage war against another country if it is believed they are developing nuclear weapons, or would it only cause more problems?

■ What do you think Sakue Shimohira would say about the development of more nuclear weapons?

A pacifist

Pacifists believe that war is never right. Bradford Lyttle is 77 years old and he has spent his life campaigning against armed conflict.

I believe that all conflict can and should be resolved through non-violent means and that any violence, anytime, anywhere, is wrong.

Don't misunderstand me – I know that there have been many tyrants throughout history who have committed unspeakably horrible crimes, it's just that I sincerely believe that armed self-defence is not the best way to oppose evil. In fact, the belief that you win by being capable of killing more people and destroying more property than your enemy is evil itself.

Bradford Lyttle is opposed to violence.

Fact bank

■ Pacifists believe that all violence is wrong, even in self-defence. Bradford Lyttle has led protests about many wars. He has even stood for election as the President of the United States to publicise his views, which were inspired by the Indian leader Mahatma Gandhi (1869–1948).

■ Gandhi and his followers resisted British rule of India through acts of non-violent civil disobedience, including refusing to obey laws and pay taxes.

Furthermore, as a pacifist I think that the very existence of chemical, biological and nuclear weapons is a danger to the world and [these weapons] have to be dismantled as quickly as possible. The longer they are around, the more chance there is of a devastating accident. And think of the money that's being spent! What a better place the world would be if it was redirected into improving people's lives rather than ending them.

Peace parade in Rome, Italy. Many people believe that a peaceful solution can be found to most problems.

Ask yourself this...

■ Is being a pacifist just a nice idea, rather than a realistic way of living? When do you think it wouldn't work?

■ Could you stand by and do nothing if someone you love was being harmed? How far do you think you would go?

■ Both Bradford Lyttle and Major Tom Fisher (see pages 8–9) would say they were "working for peace" – who is right?

Terrorism

On 12th October 2002 a bomb destroyed a nightclub in Bali, Indonesia. The testimonies below are from Amrozi bin Nurhasyim, who was sentenced to death for helping to plant the bomb, and from Erik De Haart, who was outside the club in which six of his friends were killed.

The bomber

I bought the chemicals for the bomb and the van that it was planted in. I have a pride in my heart for what happened. I am sorry for the deaths of the Balinese people, but for the white people – it serves them right, especially the Americans. But it was the only way to drive foreigners from Indonesia. They were destroying our morals; Muslim people were deserting their places of worship and turning to places of sin, like the nightclub. Let them kill me. I am happy to die a martyr. After me there will be a million more Amrozis.

Amrozi bin Nurhasyim in court.

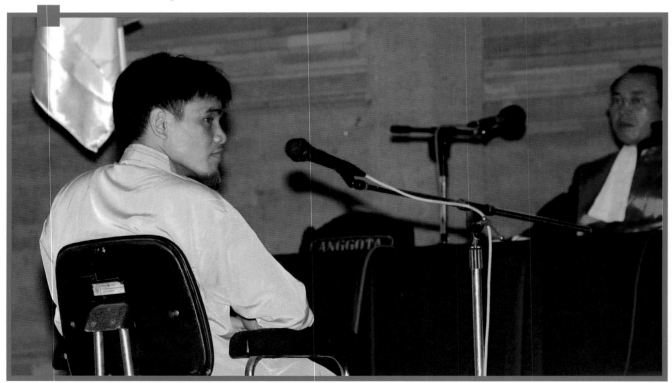

Fact bank

■ 202 citizens from 21 countries died in the Bali bombing, including 88 Australians, 38 Indonesians, 23 Britons and 7 Americans.

Some of the 202 victims of the Bali bombing.

■ The effect of terrorism is to spread fear and terror across a much wider area than just the scene of the act.

■ People who accept the terrorists' explanation for their actions consider them to be freedom fighters and, if they die, call them martyrs. Many Muslims are opposed to the use of violence.

A casualty

The best thing I can do is show those responsible that they haven't changed my life and I still live on my terms. But I really didn't want the death sentence to be passed on Amrozi bin Nurhasyim. I'd like him to be tucked in a nice, deep, dark jail somewhere and held there for the rest of his life, to suffer in the same way that all those people who lost children have suffered. But I'll never achieve closure. It will never go away. Each night I still dream about the bodies and the burned people.

Ask yourself this...

■ Do you think Amrozi bin Nurhasyim should have been sentenced to death? Why?

■ Sometimes hostages are taken by terrorists and their lives are threatened if certain demands aren't met. In such circumstances, should governments ever negotiate with terrorists? Why?

Classroom conflict

Bullying exists in some form in all schools. But teachers can only do something about it if they know it's going on. As this teacher says, it's not easy to find out the facts.

It's all very well to tell kids to report things as soon as they happen, but in my experience bullies usually wait until they are away from the glare of teachers to make their move. Break time is often the crisis-point. By the time we get to hear of it the bully has been able to come up with a plausible lie to cover his or her actions. It is so hard to know who's telling the truth. There are always two sides to an argument.

It's better for victims of bullying to talk about it.

Very often you find that the bully has been a victim themselves. They might have suffered in silence for ages, bottled up their anger and taken it out on someone "weaker". It's a vicious circle that needs to be broken.

In assembly last week the head teacher spoke about the new signs in the corridor saying "Being bullied? Speak up – don't take the law into your own hands!" We're also trying a "playground buddy" scheme, where a few of the older children get counselling training and wear special hats during break time so that a bullied child can go to them and feel safe.

Bullying can take many forms, but physical violence is often the worst.

Fact bank

Bullying is a form of conflict and can take many forms:

■ Verbal – where a bully insults or abuses their victim.

■ Physical – where a bully hits, kicks or steals from their victim.

■ Indirect – where a bully spreads rumours about their victim.

■ Direct but anonymous – by text messaging and email.

Ask yourself this...

■ Why do you think victims of physical bullying are encouraged not to hit back?

■ What are the most effective ways to "stand up" to a bully?

■ Look back through the book – what advice might the people we have met on these pages give to a bully and their victim?

What do war and conflict have to do with me?

You may have experienced war and conflict only in the cinema or in pretend playground battles. Maybe the biggest conflict in your life is over the TV remote control. Perhaps you're being bullied at home or in school. Most individuals don't have direct experience of war but, like the people quoted on these two pages, they still have opinions about it. To find out more about them look at the websites. They will also help you to answer these questions. Look back through the book, too. Use all this information to form your own opinion about war and conflict.

How easy would it be to live a totally non-violent pacifist existence?

"The chain reaction of evil – hate begetting hate, wars producing more wars – must be broken, or we shall be plunged into the dark abyss of annihilation."
  – Dr Martin Luther King Jr (Nobel peace prize-winning Civil Rights activist, 1929–68)

"There are no warlike people, just warlike leaders."
  – Ralph Bunche (Nobel peace prize-winner, 1904–71)

■ www.uspacifistparty.org
■ www.nobelprize.org/peace

What's the difference between Major Tom Fisher and a suicide bomber – after all they are both willing to die for what they believe in?

"One day we must come to see that peace is not merely a distant goal we seek, but that it is a means by which we arrive at that goal. We must pursue peaceful ends through peaceful means."
– Dr Martin Luther King Jr (Nobel peace prize-winning Civil Rights activist, 1929–68)

"It isn't poverty that breeds terrorism, but terrorism that breeds poverty."
– Dan Gillerman (UN official, born 1944)

■ www.thekingcenter.org
■ www.terrorism.com

In wars people kill each other – can that ever be right?

"So long as there are men there will be wars."
– Albert Einstein (Nobel prize-winning scientist and thinker, 1879–1955)

"The purpose of all war is ultimately peace."
– Saint Augustine (Christian leader, 354–430CE)

■ www.albert-einstein.org/
■ www.catholic-forum.com/saints/ sainta02.htm

How much is a country who picks a fight with a weaker one behaving like a playground bully?

"Looking for peace is like looking for a turtle with a moustache: You won't be able to find it."
– Ajahn Chah (Buddhist monk, 1918–92)

"If the battle for civilisation comes down to the wimps versus the barbarians, the barbarians are going to win."
– Thomas Sowell (lecturer and author, born 1930)

■ www.forestsangha.org/aboutchah.htm
■ www.tsowell.com

Websites

The websites below feature more information, news articles and stories that you can use to help form your own opinions. Use the information carefully and consider the source it comes from before drawing any conclusions.

www.un.org/peace
The "peace and security" section of the United Nations' website featuring up-to-date information on current crises, peacekeeping missions and international programmes.

www.antiwar.com
Political news-based website of the Randolph Bourne Institute. Features a wide range of up-to-date articles from countries worldwide.

www.amnesty.org
Website of Amnesty International (AI), the worldwide campaign for internationally recognised human rights. Features reports and the latest human rights news from around the world.

www.usmc.mil
Official website of the United States Marine Corps. Read more stories from serving Marines and find out about current operations.

www.childline.org.uk/ Bullying.asp
Website of Childline, the UK's 24-hour help line for children and young adults. Features advice, real stories and other resources about bullying.

http://news.bbc.co.uk/ cbbcnews
The Newsround website from the BBC featuring current news stories, including ones about war and conflict.

Glossary

Air-raid siren – loud alarm to warn people of an attack.

Ammunition – bombs and bullets fired by weapons.

Atomic bomb – a bomb that has great explosive power.

Biological weapons – weapons that spread disease.

Civilian – someone who is not a soldier.

Comrade – a close friend.

Counselling – listening to people's problems and giving helpful advice.

Deserter – a soldier who abandons his or her duty.

Deterrent – something designed to discourage an enemy from attacking.

Dismantle – to take apart.

Doomsday Clock – a picture clock that shows how close the world is to nuclear war.

Enlisting – joining.

Hostage – someone held captive against their will.

Marine – an American soldier.

Martyr – someone who is willing to sacrifice their life for what they believe in.

Nuclear weapon – see entry for atomic bomb.

Sentry duty – when a soldier stands guard.

Surrender – to stop fighting.

United Nations – an organisation that promotes peace and security.

Veteran – someone who has served in the armed forces.

Victim – a person who is harmed by someone else.

Index

War and Conflict